Warrior

*A tribute to Kevin Thompson,
the greatest sport martial artist
of all time*

Christopher M. Rappold

Mr. Media Books

FOR KEVIN AND SHENA

AND THE CHILDREN

.

CONTENTS

1. MEET KEVIN THOMPSON
BY CHRISTOPHER M. RAPPOLD

Dear Kevin,

As a 15-year-old boy, I remember seeing you fight in Boston at Rocky DiRico's tournament. I looked at you with my mouth wide open in amazement and thought, "I hope that one day I can be that good." It happened again when I was 17 years old seeing you perform your Kama form to Michael Jackson's "Smooth Criminal" and, again, I remember thinking, "I hope that one day I can be that good."

I just got off the phone hearing the news of your retirement and at 41 years old, it occurs to me that I am still thinking the same thought, "I hope that one day I can be that good" – but, of course, I know now that is impossible.

What a privilege it has been to watch you compete for the 28 years I have been in martial arts. What an honor it has been to have you as a teammate and friend. You are by far one of the greatest, most positive martial arts influences in my life and in the life of our team, Team Paul Mitchell. When God made you, he broke the mold, or, knowing you, you probably broke it yourself.

I feel a great sadness in knowing that a four decade era is coming to a close and my students who start in the future will only be treated to the stories and will not have the chance that I did to see you compete. There has never been and never will be another Kevin Thompson... "Little KA"... "The Total Package."

I feel grateful that I have had the chance to share some of the journey with you as a teammate. Thank you for your example to me of what an honorable Martial Arts Warrior is! I feel blessed to have you as a mentor, teammate and friend for life. The following tribute is offered as a sign of appreciation and respect from a sampling your friends, teammates and admirers.

Christopher Rappold
Team Member /Executive Director
Team Paul Mitchell Karate

Founder
Personal Best Karate
Norton, Massachusetts

April 2014

Christopher Rappold with Kevin Thompson, 2014

2. IN THE BEGINNING

How does one tell the story of the great Kevin Thompson?

It seems an impossible task to accurately convey in words the example of excellence Kevin's life represents. He defied the odds, broke the norms and did exactly what he shouldn't have been able to do and, in the process, inspired a generation of martial artists and admirers to strive for a level of personal and professional excellence.

Kevin's story needs to be told from the beginning so you can understand the struggles that molded the character of the man.

•••

Kevin Brown (Thompson) was born June 26, 1961, in the heart of Newark's ghetto, and he was one of seven children. His family didn't have much money and struggled to survive on welfare. His single mom did what she could, but with seven children, times were always tough. They shopped with food stamps, lining up each week to get a block of government cheese and butter, often eating mayonnaise sandwiches.

When absolutely necessary, Kevin's mom replaced his worn-out sneakers at the A&P supermarket for $1.99. "When you bought sneakers from A & P," Kevin said, "you had to be careful not to run or play too hard in them because they would tear."

New underwear came from the church on the corner of South 12th Street and 16th Avenue, priced at 15¢ per pair. A pair of socks? 5¢.

From his earliest days, Kevin's strongest influences were his older brothers, Mylo and Earl. Together they shared the role of playing big brother and father to him, since Kevin's father was not around. This was especially true of Mylo, who was 16 years older than Kevin and, being the oldest of the brothers, was handed that responsibility by his mom. She trusted Mylo while she was at work to essentially raise Kevin, treating him more like a son than a brother. And it fell to Earl to discipline Kevin when needed and hand out the household chores.

Mylo and Earl knew there was something special about Kevin, and without them, all the talents Kevin possessed would have gone unrealized. His mental focus, his discipline, his physicality and his character were all above average. When you are raised in poverty and you are one of seven, there just isn't enough to go around. In those dire circumstances, talent may simply lie dormant. Everyone needs someone to believe in him or her, to see what they don't yet see in themselves, and to craft the potential that is within. It was an absolutely certainty the world might have missed out on Kevin without his brothers.

Every child in the Thompson home was expected from a young age to help out inside and work outside to make any extra money they would like to have. Kevin? He shined shoes for 25 cents.

"Shoe shine, sir! Shoe shine, sir!" he and his friend Dennis would call out all afternoon as they positioned themselves outside the neighborhood bars to find customers coming in and out. At the end of each day they would sit together and count the money they made. On a good day they may have made $10; on some occasions, as much as $20. That was a lot of money for a child back in the 1970s.

Raised as a Christian by his mom, Kevin remembered going to church and singing his favorite song, "This Little Light of Mine." Being a bit shy, he would be the one to start the song and as soon as everyone chimed in he would stop the singing and just enjoy the melody and energy created in the room.

Tribute by DeAndre Walker

The things you have achieved in four decades of forms, weapons and sparring are remarkable and may never be duplicated. You truly are an example of hard work, sacrifice and perseverance. At the 2010 U.S. Capital Classics, I had the privilege of having lunch with you and two teammates. As you began telling us old war stories of legends, such as Steve "Nasty" Anderson, Billy Blanks and a few others, I felt as if I were present during those fights. Your energy and passion made me realize why I enjoy training and competing at the highest level.

-- DeAndre Walker, member of Team Paul Mitchell Karate

Tribute by Steve Babcock

I had the honor of being a teammate with Kevin on Team Paul Mitchell. Not only was I his teammate but for most of the time we roomed with each other.

To me Kevin is the ultimate martial artist. He believed that to be the best fighter you had to be able to do kata and to be the best at kata you also have to fight. A true martial artist thinks these things complement each other. Not only was Kevin able to do these things, he was number one in his division competitively for most of his long 40-year career.

Kevin was the type of person that didn't handle losing well – but what champion does? I'm not saying he was a sore loser. Quite the contrary, he would be tough on himself when he didn't win. He would always say, "I've got to work on this more. Or, maybe instead of competing with my kamas, I'll use the sword." It's this quality that allows a person to compete 40 years in competition but never really getting old. Kevin always loved the challenge.

We always talk to our students about a martial artist as not only a role model in the dojo but that he or she is a role model with their friends and the community. As a friend, Kevin brought those qualities to the table and more. Kevin and I were usually by each other's side

*during our years of competing because we shared the
same ring, just in different divisions. When our day was
done we would go back to the room and discuss ways of
improving or recalling the things we did particularly
well. We shared our life stories with each other, good
and bad. That's when his friendship was even more of a
role model than his competition. We made each other
laugh and sometimes, when I needed to hear things I
didn't want to hear, Kevin would tell me anyway, which
is what a true friend does.*

*I pride myself on what type of martial artist I am for
my friends, family, and community. Whatever grade I
would give myself, I would always give Kevin
Thompson a higher one on all levels and I think most
people who know him would do the same.*

-- Steve Babcock, co-founder of Team Paul Mitchell Karate

3. STARTING KARATE

Mylo was, without a doubt, the biggest influence in introducing Kevin to karate training. After Mylo himself began training, he invested his time and energy in teaching Kevin, then five years old, in the Thompson home. For two years, Mylo trained Kevin privately in the skills he learned from his own lessons. When Kevin was seven, Mylo brought him into the karate school to train with his Sensei, the famous Kareem Abdullah.

Sensei's influence was profound. A devout Muslim, he preached a life of clean living: no alcohol, no drugs, and that one always must show respect to the elderly, women and children and, above all, pursue hard physical training. With two years of home training, Kevin progressed much faster than the typical beginner and sped his journey to becoming a Black Belt.

But it was far from easy. In those days, Sensei's academy was a *fighting* school. Students learned how to fight, quite frankly, by getting beat up.

Every day, Kevin ran home from school to let his mom know he was okay and then it was off to the studio. He did his homework and was taught about life and living through the mentoring of older students in the school.

Jerry Stewart was the teen that helped Kevin with his homework. Reginald Williams, another teen, disciplined Sensei's younger students and tutored them in etiquette. Together with Tanya Hill and another student – Bryant -- they all worked together to mold Kevin's behavior and ensured he kept up in martial arts, the classroom and life in general.

Hard training in the backyard of the dojo on Springfield Avenue in North New Jersey. In the background, Robert Wright (Mr. Graceful), and in front, 14-year-old Kevin Thompson.

At the time, the goal in karate training was to grab your partner, sweep him to the ground and start punching him. From there it was the student's responsibility to fight his way up from the mat. A student named Saladine was more advanced than Kevin and put a beating on the younger boy at every class meeting. But Kevin, being a fast learner, didn't let much time pass before he turned the tables and Saladine found himself on the receiving end of the daily punishment.

As Kevin often said, there is something that separates the great from the mediocre. The great meet their challenges head on and *NEVER* give up.

Besides his daily routine, Kevin remembered a time when his brother Mylo (who paid for Kevin's lessons) was away in the Air Force Reserves and returned to find that Kevin had stopped attending karate classes. Kevin had given into being an eight-year-old and decided instead to stay home and relax.

That was a mistake.

In Kevin's house, karate training was not an option, it was what the brothers *did*. When Mylo returned home from his military service and found his younger brother out, "He whipped me half to death," Kevin said.

Mylo told Kevin in no uncertain terms, "I am paying for your lessons. If you ever miss another day, I will kill you."

That was an example of the tough love that all the Thompson siblings had for one another. They knew it was only through a disciplined life that they would have the chance to succeed.

Tribute by Jackson Rudolph

Most martial artists have heard the old cliché, "Martial Arts is not just a sport, but a way of life." Many people disregard this and continue on with their hobby and go home unchanged. At the same time, there are the people who take what they learn and apply it to their lives outside of the Dojo.

Kevin Thompson is the perfect example of one of those people. Not only did he achieve extraordinary goals in the realm of competition, he took all of the principles that are taught in the martial arts and used those to become a great person as well as a great competitor.

First, I have to reflect on the outstanding competitor he was.

In sport karate today, you basically have two categories of competitors: the forms people and the fighters. Rarely do you see a talent great enough to do both. Occasionally a fighter will compete in one or two forms divisions, and maybe a forms competitor fights just for fun, but people are rarely serious about doing both.

Kevin Thompson was successful at both for a vast majority of his career. His versatility was matched by few people in sport karate's history. Not only was he versatile, he was entertaining. He was, for the most part, a traditionalist, which in most cases is a competitor that is clean and strong in all of the basic techniques and competes just in traditional divisions.

Most people are not excited when watching any traditional form, except for when it was Kevin Thompson. He brought so much energy into everything he did that he could probably have run a White Belt's form and still have been impressive. He gave it everything he had even when there was no one for him to compete against. I watched him several times in the 30-and-over division at the end of his career and most of the time no one could touch him, but he never played down to his competition. If he was going to run a form, it was going to be his best.

Second, is about the kind of person that I see him to be.

The first time I ever talked to Kevin was at the U.S. Open in 2009. His son did not have a bo staff to compete with Friday night, so he asked if his son could use mine. Awestruck that someone like Kevin Thompson would even look in my direction, I, of course, told him, "Yes, sir." As he walked away I still couldn't believe that he had even talked to me, but that is the kind of person Mr. Thompson is. It is almost like he doesn't realize who he is. His ego is entirely nonexistent. That's where the principles of martial arts come into play; he is humble. He is also extremely respectful and polite. Shaking hands with whoever wanted to meet him or talk to him, always with a smile on his face.

When we spoke, he called me "Sir," said "Please" and "Thank you," and made me feel like I was doing this incredible thing just by letting his son borrow a bo.

I have been able to study the way he competed and the way he carried himself and could learn from him just by watching from a distance. I look up to him a lot because of this and will never forget about him.

I will pass Kevin's story on to future generations of competitors so that he can always have the positive effects that he had on me and on the rest of the sport karate community. Just as martial arts is more than a sport — it is a way of life — Kevin Thompson was more than an athlete, he was a role model, the perfect definition of a martial artist.

Jackson Rudolph, member of Team Paul Mitchell Karate

4. IMMERSION — AND THE CREATION OF "LITTLE K.A."

If Kevin Thompson thought his experience of training was intense up to that point in life he was about to experience a whole other level of immersion.

In 1973, Kevin's house caught on fire and burned to the point of being uninhabitable. As a result, his siblings were split up and stayed with family members and friends until their home was repaired. Kevin asked his mom if he could stay with Sensei Kareem, who lived at his school. She said yes. He was now surrounded by martial arts all day, every day.

Kevin's instructor often woke him up in the middle of the night and said, "Hey, come here, I got a new way of blocking a punch," or "I have a new self-defense move I want to try out."

This was one of the ways that Kevin experienced the evolution of the Kareem Abdullah (KA) system. It was through experimentation, then battle testing in the school, in a tournament, or on the street that Kareem Abdullah developed and perfected his system. Being a part of that process increased Kevin's discipline and made him stronger over the year and a half he lived with Sensei.

Kevin became known as "Little K.A.," named after his instructor for his fierce training and competitive spirit. This was demonstrated when, at the age of 10, he was ready to test for his Black Belt. In 1972, a 10-year-old testing for his Black Belt was so unusual that posters were made and hung around town. On the poster it read: "Will this young 10-year-old kid make Black Belt?"

Sure enough, he did.

•••

The seven children in Kevin's family shared the same mom but came from different dads and, as a result, each brother had a different last name. In the early years of attending tournaments, Kevin and his brothers all used Mylo's last name — Thompson — to avoid confusion and it created a unifying front for the family. For the record, Kevin's last name at birth was "Brown," although the world knows him as Kevin Thompson.

When Kevin was 12 years old in 1973, he competed in sparring against his age group and Kata against grown adult men. At Fred Hamilton's Invitational in New York City, Kevin went head-to-head in Kata competition with Earl Bennett, who was a great competitor in his mid-twenties and was the teacher of Billy Beason, who would later become Kevin's own toughest competition. Kevin and Mr. Bennett performed their routine and the scores were tied twice. The tradition in those days was thant if the score were tied, each competitor would perform a different kata. Unfortunately for Kevin, he only knew two. But Kevin thought quickly and presented himself again and he performed a routine that creatively combined the two katas he knew together. The crowd was so awed by his performance that they stood up and cheered. At the age of 12, Kevin did something he wasn't expected to do and maybe had never been done before; he won the Overall Grand Championship for *all* ages.

Kevin trained with Sensei through 1975 when, after losing to the World Kickboxing champion at the time, Sensei decided to devote himself totally to boxing. Kevin followed him all the way to the 8th Street Boxing Gym, training and competing in the Golden Gloves 128-132 weight division. Short and stocky, Kevin came up against an extremely tall fighter in the third round that was able to keep him away with his jab. This frustrated Kevin because his martial arts muscle memory saw the openings and wanted to kick to offset this opponent's long reach but he was not able to according to the rules.

"If I could have kicked him or grabbed him and swept him down to the ground," Kevin said years later, "it would have been a whole lot different. I thought, 'This guy can't beat me.'"

Feeling physically contained, Kevin wanted to go right back to his martial arts training. After the match, he went to his brother Earl and said, "I don't want to limit myself to just boxing, I want to go back to karate." His brother saw the passion in his eyes and agreed to bring him to Sensei to tell him of Kevin's decision.

Sensei refused to go along with Kevin's wishes, so when he was in 10th grade, student and Sensei parted ways.

Tribute by Alex Lane

You have given all of our teammates a reason to keep our guards tight, to stay strong and ultimately be the best we can be. As I look back over the years, I know for a fact that if ever I doubted myself or questioned my potential, I would always remind myself, "What would K.A. do?" I thank the man upstairs for all the times we had together as teammates. You are my mentor, my teammate, and, above all, my hero.

Alex Lane, member of Team Paul Mitchell Karate

5. BASKETBALL AND THE MAKING OF A LIFELONG FRIEND

Attitude among the children in the Thompsons' neighborhood was critical to survival.

Kevin and his brothers ruled the hood and established a reputation for not being easily pushed around. If someone went after one brother, all the brothers stood up to protect their kin. Unity kept them strong and sent a strong message to anyone that you didn't mess with the Thompsons.

Playing basketball in the street, young men needed skill and to be able to "sell your noise" — in other words, trash talk. Games were physical and there was endless pushing and shoving.

One of the boys Kevin often played against was Mike Glover.

In one particular game, Mike was getting the best of one of Kevin's teammates, Myron. In the middle of a play, Mike fouled Myron but Mike didn't respect the call. Kevin immediately went into protection mode for his teammate; disrespect was not allowed if Kevin was around. He grabbed Mike by the shirt but before the first punch hit, Kevin's teammate, Myron, yelled, "Kevin, don't hit him!"

Mike's mind had flashed across images of the posters around town of Little K.A. as a 10-year-with a Black Belt. Mike was relieved he didn't get hit, but didn't feel Kevin was finished with him.

The next day, Kevin sought out Mike at school. When Mike saw Kevin walking toward him, he expected the worst
Mike was pleasantly surprised to hear Kevin ask, "Do you want to be on my basketball team?"

The "noise" from the previous day aside, Kevin respected Mike's playing ability and knew that having Mike on *his* team would be an asset. That started a relationship that became Kevin's most enduring. Mike became his best and closest friend for life.

Kevin continued his martial arts training even as he improved his basketball skills, earning spots on Barringer High School's junior varsity and Newark Tech's varsity teams. Although it was a different discipline, Kevin brought the same level of attention and competitiveness to hoops. And at only 5'4", he once again proved that heart mattered more than height. His ball handling skills and awareness of the court made him an All-Star in this arena as well.

He went on to play at Essex County College in 1979 under the great basketball coach Cleo "Black Magic" Hill and, as the team's starting point guard, contributed much to the team's overall success.

In 1980, Kevin was a student athlete at Rutgers University in New Brunswick, New Jersey, where he studied business and marketing. He played basketball for the Scarlet Knights but, in a freak accident, he went up for a rebound during fall basketball practice, came down and twisted his ankle and ruptured his ligaments on landing. As a result, Kevin was in a cast that went from his ankle halfway up his thigh. That injury ended his year playing basketball, cost him his partial scholarship, and due to financial reasons forced him to withdraw from Rutgers.

Tribute by Preston Clements

You are an inspiration and a true competitor in life and the martial arts. You have been a great team captain over the years and were always there to motivate your teammates. I am proud to have been on the same team as you wearing the black and white.

Preston Clements, member of Team Paul Mitchell Karate

6. OPENING A DOJO AND BECOMING
A TEACHER AT 19

Sensei Kareem Abdullah closed his martial arts school in 1975, shortly after his full contact World Championship loss.

It was always a goal of Kevin Thompson's that one day he would open up a school of his own and carry on the "K.A." system and traditions.

One day in March 1981, on a walk to the store, Kevin came across a vacant space to rent. "This," he thought, "would be the perfect place for the K.A. School of Martial Arts."

Though it was a mess when he found it, Kevin knew with a little cleanup it would make a perfect space to open his own school. The landlord, Sam Allen, gave Kevin the space for free to start on the promise that Kevin would invest his own time and money — "sweat equity" — to clean it up. Always true to his word, Kevin worked tirelessly to fulfilling his promise.

When he had done his part, Kevin went back to Allen and asked him how much the rent would now be.

"You don't even have any students yet," Allen said. "Why don't you sign up some students first and then we can talk about how much rent I will charge you."

A year went by and Kevin successfully built up a base of dedicated students, still not knowing the price of rent. Again he returned to Sam Allen and asked how much the rent would be.

"How about $300 per month?" Allen said.

Kevin was amazed at how generous Allen was in ensuring he could afford the price. He went home and immediately told his brother Earl the great news. With Earl's help and guidance, Kevin lived his dream and taught the "K.A. System" of martial arts and passed on the knowledge

Earl Brown and Kevin in front of Kevin's first dojo at 362 South Park St.
Newark, New Jersey

that had so profoundly shaped his life.

In 1983, Kevin paid tribute to his former Sensei by hosting a banquet in his honor. The planning for the evening was extensive. Celebrity guests were invited, including famed International Boxing Federation referee Larry Hazard and the 1982 New England Patriots second round draft pick Andre Tippett. Both Hazard and Tippett grew up in Newark, NJ, and were friends with Kevin.

The night was filled with speeches and martial arts demonstrations from Kevin and his students. He awarded his Sensei with a plaque in honor of his contributions to the sport. It had been eight years since Sensei closed his school and left the martial arts. He never saw the continual training and natural progression of the martial arts system he once taught. He missed the evolution and improvement of the system, so this night was set to be a proud showcase by Kevin to display the work he had done in keeping his teacher's legacy alive.

When the evening drew to a close, Kevin thanked Sensei for coming. But he sensed a tension — something was not right. Sensei was mad at Kevin.

"That's *not* the K.A. system," he said angrily.

Sensei demanded Kevin change the name of his school, insisting it bear no trace of Sensei Kareem Abdullah's influence or name. Kevin was shocked and heartbroken at the displeasure of the man who meant so much to him following an evening he personally arranged to honor and respect the man's legacy and contributions to the martial arts.

Change the school's name? And to what?

Kevin specifically opened the school to carry on the teachings of his Sensei and named the school appropriately. Now, he had been ordered to change the name even though his entire professional and personal identities were wrapped in the K.A. System. The people in New York called him, "The little warrior from across the river." And his Islamic name, Shakil, when translated means "The Willing One. The one whose willpower is strong enough to go beyond the stopping point." What a stopping point he absorbed from his Sensei!

After much thought and consideration, Kevin changed the name of the school to his Islamic name. Moving forward, the school would be called "Shakil's School of Martial Arts" and its students would be "Shakil's Warriors." There is a rumor that the great NBA basketball star and National Collegiate Basketball Hall of Famers Shaquille O'Neal's name was inspired by Kevin's name, Shakil. Though spelled different, Shaq played in the game Boys and Girls Club at the same time that Kevin was active within their community.

Tribute by Kalman Csoka

You are truly a legend. Thank you for inspiring me when I was little and a new competitor all the way through till now. Thank you for always being such an amazing role model for this team and the circuit.

Kalman Csoka, member of Team Paul Mitchell Karate

7. COMPETITION

Trips around the world brought ever-greater tests of Kevin's skills but also strained his personal life.

Kevin met Lisa at Bloomfield College in 1982. They graduated together four years later and Lisa gave birth to their daughter, Shana, the same year. In 1988, they were married. But with all of the traveling and demands placed on Kevin and, as a result of his growing popularity in the international martial arts scene, his home life suffered. Kevin and Lisa divorced in 1993.

•••

Kevin and his brother Earl were frequently invited overseas to put on seminars to martial arts students and to compete in their tournaments. European martial artists first took their full measure of Kevin's talents at the 1987 world championships.

It was in London, England, in 1985 at Barris Sweeney's All-England Championship that Kevin gave one of his most memorable performances ever.

As usual, the fighting divisions were broken up in weight classes: super light, light, light middle, middle light heavy, and heavy.

Kevin went against Europe's best fighter in the lightweight division and came out on top. As is customary, all the winners of each division fight at the end to determine the event's grand champion. Kevin won his bracket, beating the super lightweight and light middleweight winners, while at the other end of the bracket was the famous light heavyweight world champion Kevin Brewerton.

Since Brewerton was the returning champion, he did not have to fight through his divisions as Kevin did; he simply waited until it was narrowed down to a final competitor, whom he fought for the Overall Grand Championship.

Training session with teammate and extraordinary super lightweight
fighter Tony Young at the Atlantic training camp in Connecticut,
circa 1992

According to Kevin's brother Earl, the tension in the crowd built as
it appeared the two Kevins would meet each other in the final match to
determine who was the day's best.

Brewerton had a size and strength advantage, a weight advantage
and a hometown advantage, all of which concerned Kevin. Being from
England, he had an entire country in his corner as he prepared to do away
with the American lightweight. The match was two, two-minute rounds
with the person scoring the most points at the end of the match declared
the winner.

As everyone predicted, Brewerton jumped out to a commanding

four-point lead in the first round. It looked like he was headed for yet another win. When Kevin came back to the corner, his brother Earl smacked him on his butt.

"Kevin, what are you doing?" Earl asked. "Get out there and beat this guy! He can't hang with you! Go forward and take the fight to him! You have to be first!"

Whether it was the words or just something Kevin innately knew, he lined up for the start of round two. When the bell rang Kevin rallied for eight consecutive points by taking the fight to the bigger Brewerton with a series of blitzes.

Frustrated and with only 8 seconds left, Brewerton threw off his gloves and took a fighting stance. This was his way of sending a message to the little lightweight from the U.S. that he was lucky this wasn't a *real* fight. To everyone's surprise, especially Brewerton, Kevin threw off *his* gloves and took a matching stance, preparing to finish off the bigger Brewerton.

Brewerton dropped his guard and the time expired.

Kevin ran around the ring with his finger raised in victory, yelling "USA! USA! USA!" The crowd was so impressed with his performance that they began chanting it along with him.

Tribute by Marc Canonizado

It was an honor to be on the same team with such an amazing legendary martial artist. Growing up as a kid, I would watch you fight and, of course, do your katas because it amazed me that someone could have such raw power. Your legacy will always be present at every single tournament. A great memory I have of you was when a few of us had the opportunity to head to Camp Woodward. That was the first time I had the chance to say that I did demos with the great Kevin Thompson. Performing with you was great, but by far the best part was getting to know you and your family.

Marc Canonizado, member of Team Paul Mitchell, Actor

8. LOVE AT FIRST SIGHT

One afternoon, a beautiful young woman from Bermuda named Shena walked into Kevin's school.

Shena was curious about martial arts training for her son, whom she said was back home in Bermuda. She asked a lot of questions about classes. Kevin asked whether she had any interest in taking lessons herself and extended unlimited, free training so she could try it out first hand. He even called Shena every other day to encourage her interest in his offer. (Kevin says that was his standard business procedure but *Shena* says it was the beginning of Kevin's courtship of her.) Shena took classes and did well.

Prior to heading back to Bermuda, Kevin invited Shena to dinner. This was the start of a great friendship and eventually a wonderful and enduring marriage.

Shena's dedication to Kevin was profound. It started with small things, such as bringing him lunch at the karate school before they were married and continued as she encouraged him to fulfill his potential. The relationship was just what Kevin needed to excel personally the way he always did on the martial arts stage.

Proud family man: Kevin with his wife Sheena, daughter KeShea, and Kevin Junior (KJ) in Springfield, New Jersey, in 2002

Tribute by Elias Lemon

I can't even begin to tell you what an inspiration you have been to me throughout the years. Since the time I was an under belt you have had a major impact on martial arts and all those around you. I can only hope that someday I can inspire others like you have inspired me.

Elias Lemon, member of Team Paul Mitchell Karate

Tribute by Greg Betlach

The memory I will always have of Kevin is the first team meeting in which I was involved. Everyone warned me about his handshake. Alex Lane pushed me in front of Kevin, and my hand has never been the same. What I found that day and subsequent years later was that Kevin has that same tenacity, intensity and passion in all of the things he does.

Thank you, Kevin, for being such an inspiration and role model. The impression you have on this team and in the marital arts world can never be duplicated.

Simply put, thank you for yourself.

Greg Betlach, member of Team Paul Mitchell Karate

9. A COLLEGE GRADUATE AT LAST

Kevin always believed that he would be a college graduate.

He prided himself on being an educated man and setting an example for his children. The first college he graduated from — with a Bachelor's degree in Marketing — was Bloomfield College. He was a student by day and ran his martial arts took a management position with an ambulance company, giving him responsibility for managing as many as 15 vehicles.

The job lasted about a year, until he received a call from his friend Larry Hazzard. Larry was a principal at Broadway Middle School in Newark and wanted to improve the climate of the school.

"I only know one guy who can help me with what I want to do with the schools," he told Kevin. "I will bring you in as a substitute teacher to start. You will need to get an emergency certificate to allow you to become a full-time permanent teacher."

Kevin went to Keane College to take the six courses needed to work full-time at University High School, where he was on the teaching staff for three years. From there he went to Barringer High School in 1990. Three years later, Kevin was promoted to the position of "crisis" teacher, helping special needs children as well as the general student population for the next 17 years. In this position, Kevin instituted a variety of proactive programs that gave troubled children the help and support they needed. He created a peer leadership program and provided seminars and professional development to fill some of the gaps he saw. Kevin's effort was a massive success; it would be hard to measure how many lives were saved as a result of his programs.

In 2010, Kevin earned a Master's degree and became vice principal at Barringer High School, where he worked until retirement in 2013.

Tribute by Julie Solwold

You embody the heart, soul and integrity of the team. You demand excellence from yourself and make those around you raise our own expectations to match yours, you make us better. Better team members, better competitors, better family members and better souls. The team was blessed to be led by your wisdom for so long. I was blessed to share your friendship for so long.

Julie Solwold is vice president of sports marketing for Paul Mitchell Systems

10. APPLYING GOD'S GIFTS

Kevin Thompson was always a fierce competitor. He consistently beat his foes thanks to a superior strategy and an unmatched physicality.

As with all of the greats, Kevin did everything within his power to overcome his own weaknesses and expose those of his opponents. He studied his opponents the way a football coach studies the next team he will face. He learned from everyone around him, took what was useful and discarded the rest.

Kevin's singular mindset was on winning the day's match and doing so within the rules of the sport. On occasion, when tempers flared and a competitor tried ratcheting up the match a notch or two beyond what the rules allowed, Kevin always put them in check.

He had a reputation for always treating his fellow competitors fairly, even as he aggressively played the sport. If you hit him hard you knew you would get hit back at least as hard, just like it was in his early days of playing pick-up street hoops. Spectators saw him and thought him fierce, a force of nature, but Kevin did it all without ever having hate in his heart. Hatred of others was forbidden for Muslims, he would point out. If he knew he was significantly superior to an opponent, Kevin went easy on his foe. He never took advantage of someone.

Kevin always appreciated his God-given gifts. He believed the Creator allowed him the success he had.

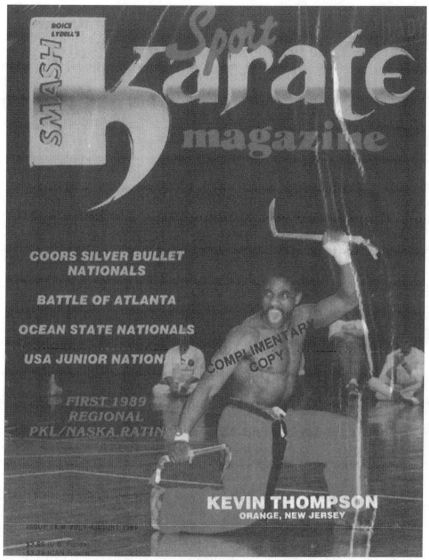

Kevin Thompson on the front cover of Boyce Lydell's
Sport Karate Magazine in 1989

Tribute by Mike Pombiero

I first saw Kevin Thompson at a tournament in Boston. I was about 15 years old and I had just started to hit the bigger tournaments. I saw Kevin do both his traditional form as well as his kamas and was very impressed. He was intense, had really strong stances and great charisma. What really impressed me though was when he put on the sparring pads.

I first saw him fight against one of the Brady brothers. I knew the Bradys well, as well as their talents. Kevin's ability to fake and work around one of the Bradys attacks impressed me immensely. They went back and forth. There was a point at which they gave each other a staredown and Kevin patted Brady on the butt and said, "Let's do this." Brady repeated what Kevin said in a sarcastic tone. The only problem was Kevin didn't like it and told him, "Let's do this outside, you little punk." The refs and other Black Belts helped break them up. In the end, Kevin won and moved on to the next round.

In the next round, Kevin had to face Pedro Xavier. As for a guy not only from my era but also once again being from the East Coast, Pedro was like a sparring God to us out there, so I couldn't wait to watch this fight. Kevin's intensity was ridiculous, as was his warrior spirit. Pedro and Kevin went at it back and forth. I felt like the match went on for about five minutes. They also got into a few altercations during the match. One time, Kevin walked towards the door, taking off his pads saying to Pedro, "Let's do this outside, punk, in the parking lot." By the looks of it, Pedro wanted no part of that. I couldn't believe Kevin challenged Pedro like that in his own backyard. He had no fear and believed immensely in his talents. Kevin won the match against Pedro.

I watched Kevin more and more as I started to travel. There's one thing I will never forget learning from watching and talking to him — I still do it to this day. He had this move he would do, not only on Pedro who was a great kicker, but to many of the great fighters. He had an incredible fake that he would make his opponent bite on. Then, when he bit on it, Kevin would angle change to the side and make the other guy miss. He could get around or through anyone.

I am deeply saddened by the news of his illness and keep him in my daily prayers. He has left a big hole in the sport. No one has his intensity and those looks that could kill. He could crush your hand with a handshake. People avoided him so they wouldn't get beaten up just saying "Hi" to him. He is loved and close to my heart!!!

Mike Pombiero, member of Team Paul Mitchell Karate

11. "THE TOTAL PACKAGE"

To go into a martial arts event and compete in all three divisions is like asking someone else to win a 400-yard dash, a boxing match and a baseball hitting contest in the same day... it is virtually impossible to do.

Most martial artists specialize. They devote 100 percent of their time to one event and then go to tournaments with a singular focus. Kevin was the rare martial artist who divided his time among all three divisions. This should have put him at a significant disadvantage since he had two-thirds less time than others to focus on each.

Kevin was in Montreal competing as usual in all three divisions: fighting, forms and weapons. He was up against the best that North America and the world had to offer.

It was an Official Atlantic Team Event, which meant the highest level of talent in every division would be represented. Each division that Kevin created in would put him face-to-face with the world's best.

"It's your competition that makes you great," Kevin said, reflecting on his achievements. And on this day, make no doubt, he *would* be tested.

Kevin competed against legendary Canadian Forms Champion Jean Frenette (who went on to great success as a stunt performer and coordinator in movies such as *X-Men: Days of Future Past* and TV series such as "Warehouse 13," "Nikita," "Covert Affairs" and "Man Seeking Woman"), as well as brothers Ho-Sung Pak (who performed in the Mortal Kombat and Mortal Kombat II video games and the "WMAC Masters" TV series) and Hoyoung Pak (who performed stunts in the original *Teenage Mutant Ninja Turtles II: The Secret of the Ooze* and *Teenage Mutant Ninja Turtles III* movies), Keith Cooke Hirabayashi

(*Beverly Hills Ninja, Mortal Kombat, Mortal Kombat: Annihilation*), and probably the greatest traditional Japanese Forms competitor of his era, Domingo Llaos.

MALE CO-COMPETITOR OF THE YEAR

Kevin Thompson

Kevin Thompson was named *Black Belt Magazine*'s "Co-competitor of the Year" in 1989

Domingo Llanos.

To say in forms and weapons he went up against the best would be an understatement. On this day, Kevin went up against many men who were and are still considered the very best ever to compete in the field.

And yet... Kevin won first place in each of his divisions, including the defeat of one of the fastest fighters to ever put on hand and feet pads, super lightweight Tony Young. This, in and of itself, made for an amazing day.

During the night finals, Kevin found himself in direct competition for the grand championship in each division against people who would be found on any list of the sport's all-time greats.: Mike Bernado, perhaps the greatest weapons competitor to ever perform with a Bo staff; Hoyoung Pak, and Steve "Nasty" Anderson, considered by many to be the greatest sport karate fighter of all time who, during the day, beat the great Billy Blanks (who later went on to fame and fortune by creating the Tae Bo phenomenon).

Each competitor was focused on beating Kevin; Kevin was focused on beating all three of them.

Imagine the swelling drama as he beat his first competitor, Canadian-born Bernado, who dropped his weapon during his performance.

In the second division, he faced Pak, who tied Kevin twice. But Kevin finally defeated him by pulling out a more basic brown belt form that he presented with unparalleled precision and intensity to win the forms grand prize as well.

Finally, Kevin was face-to-face with Anderson, a brilliant, 6-foot, 3-inch, 220-pound fighter who prided himself on never having lost to lightweights. He never had the chance to do harm to Kevin Thompson, who handily beat him that day.

For someone to win three grand championships in one day was almost unheard of. And to win three grand championships against the caliber of talent of those three specific competitors had never before been done and will never be duplicated. It was this performance and many like it that gave Kevin's nickname an adult update: "The Total Package."

Tribute by Grandmaster Dennis Brown

When I think of Kevin Thompson, I always think of a Warrior. He displays the true martial spirit of Yin and Yang, someone who speaks softly and at the same time greets you with a handshake that can easily break every bone in your hand. Kevin always reminded us all of how the true martial artist should live.

In my opinion, "Kevin Thompson is the 8th Wonder of the World.

Grandmaster Dennis Brown is promoter of the U.S. Capital Classics

12. THE TRAINING RITUALS OF A CHAMPION

If you had the opportunity to peek behind the curtain of a legend in any sport, what you would discover is a disciplined approach to preparation. And while some may copy parts of the routine for a few weeks or a few months, Kevin Thompson kept his routine up for more than 40 years.

"Please give me strength, power and will, and to stay strong and to work as hard as I can."

Kevin's personal Dua (prayer) was recited at the start of every practice or competition. He used this simple, humble statement to get himself engaged in his personal training routine.

After the Dua, Kevin hopped on a treadmill for 15 to 20 minutes. He always did this first, in part to get the energy flowing and get mentally and physically in practice mode. It started out at a jog and progressively grew faster. He was after the natural burst of energy the exercise created.

Once his muscles were warm from running, Kevin began a 15-minute stretching routine that ensured his muscles had the proper range of motion so he could execute what followed at his highest level. Next was core and upper body fitness strength and conditioning, which included 100 full sit-ups and 100 full push-ups (chest and chin to the floor). Each push-up set was done with a different hand position to work different muscles and ensure his body was ready for battle.

At the completion of this, Kevin began his Kata routine, a set of 50 to 100 prearranged movements combining deep stances, kicks, punches, blocks and strikes, all timed with total intensity and exacting precision. Kevin's decision on which routine to use was always made at the end of a previous season, based on performance, competition and wins. It was

Kevin on the front cover of *Martial Arts Training Magazine*
with Nigel Binns

that one routine that was selected and then practiced every training session for an entire year.

"If it ain't, broke don't fix it," Kevin would say, meaning that if the Kata has been a consistent winner all year, then it transferred over to the subsequent year. If that was the decision, then the focus was purely to go to work on making it even better.

The Kata was performed 10 times from beginning to end with only a minute or two break in-between. The practice started slow and precise and then gained speed, always with careful attention paid to define each and every movement. With the last three times, performances were done with the same level of competition, timing and intensity.

Next was his weapons routine. He repeated the same steps 10 times process, starting slowly and building the detail, speed, timing and power into it so that by the end, Kevin was satisfied with the progress he made in his performance.

While this was already more than what most martial arts competitors would do in a single workout, Kevin moved next to fighting drills. He would select a particular kick/punch combination and work it 10 times on the left side and 10 times on the right side. He practiced the physical discipline of both left and right side execution to keep his body even and in balance, even though he would only apply it on one side in competition.

A key philosophy in Kevin's training was always being over-prepared so that his body, mind and spirit were prepared for whatever happened.

Kevin took this same left-side/right-side discipline and applied it to five of the kick/punch combinations he was likely to use in a competition. Each was practiced in front of a mirror so he could see his exact position and get a clear view of what his opponent would see. Some of the sample combinations he favored included:

- Front leg hook kick, roundhouse kick, step down, blitz
- Front leg low high roundhouse kick, step down, blitz
- Fake ax sidekick, step down, blitz
- Just blitzing both sides
- Front leg high/low roundhouse kick, blitz
- Straight back kicks

Even though Kevin was known for his amazingly timed and powerful punches, he always believed that he needed to have the best precision and conditioning to rely on his legs if needed.

At the end of mirror work, Kevin moved on to a water-filled heavy bag for five, three-minute rounds using both hands and feet. This was where he practiced hitting with explosive power — his fighting trademark. At the end of the heavy bag training, it was back to the floor for 100 more full sit-ups and chest and chin to the floor push-ups.

His training also extended to heavy training on the Makiwara, a canvas pad attached to a cement wall that Kevin used to condition his punches, forearms and palm heels. He also believed in grip strength, as anyone who had ever shaken his hand would remember. Kevin had a bucket of sand and gravel in his dojo that he would punch and stir 50 times with each hand. Through years of conditioning, the gravel and sand would end up turning into a fine powder.

Finally, to end the physical workout, Kevin unwound with a five- to 10-minute meditation. He did this while he was still in a peak physical state of mind so he could attain clarity. He sat and listened to tapes from his "oldies but goodies" collection including The Temptations, The Stylistics, The Manhattans and The Delphonics as a way of relaxing and feeling good.

He used this same routine on tournament days. He imagined himself waiting at the airport dressed in a suit and tie, after leaving work, to board the plane. He pictured himself getting off the airplane in some distant city, walking through the airport and getting on a shuttle that would take him to the venue. He pictured the people he would see in the airport, on the shuttle, or in the event hotel lobby.

Kevin always believed he was taken better care of and more respected when he dressed the part of a successful person and he was right. In most cases he was coming straight from work so it was easy to maintain a professional image throughout his travels. That meant the discipline to avoid doing simple things such as not unbuttoning his top button until the plane took off. It was an extension of his personal discipline.

Kevin adhered to and sustained a standard of excellence, supported by predictable rituals, that gave him the feeling — and others the image— that he was a professional athlete. It was his unwavering standard.

Everything he did was practiced and visually rehearsed so that Kevin's aura and performance inside and outside the ring spoke of a standard that was a cut above the norm. He visualized who would be at the competition and against whom he would compete. He saw himself on stage at the night finals and accepting the Grand Championship trophy. He calculated the money he would win at the conclusion of a day's events and pictured calling home to let his family know how well he had done.

Everything he did was the product of two creations: first, in his mind, and second, in the physical world. Kevin created his own reality at the end of every practice session — three to four times per week, and up to two and a half hours per session for four decades. And this did not include the additional drills and training he did with his martial arts school students three days per week.

Kevin extended his training to holidays as well. He used them as another tool to separate himself from the competition. He knew that nine out of 10 of the people he would compete against would be lax in their training on those days. Kevin, however, used those days to turn up the heat on himself.

"Let everyone else take the day off," he told himself. "I am going to use this as a day to get ahead of them. I will enjoy the day *after* my training is complete. My training will be done while my competition is still in bed."

Another element of his routine was calling his long-time friend, Anthony Arango, on the phone every holiday to tell him he was training and to make sure Anthony was doing the same.

Kevin's discipline extended to nutrition as well. His brother Earl once told him, "When you eat meat it gives you meanness and toughness, it gives you the ripping and tearing." Whether true or not, Kevin took the idea and created a diet mostly centered on fruits and vegetables, adding meat sparingly, except for a steak the week of an event.

His daily nutrition consisted of a smoothie in the morning mostly made with bananas, strawberries, grapes and apples. Lunch was light: usually a small sandwich on wheat bread with an apple or orange and a bottle of water was all he needed. Dinner was bigger. Typical meals included fish, chicken, broccoli, corn on the cob and pasta.

The week of an event, Kevin would add complex carbs on a Wednesday and Thursday to give him sustained energy that he would need to perform in all of his divisions. On Friday, the day of competition, he usually consumed a smoothie for breakfast, a small serving of pasta, a light lunch, and some cashews and raisins or a fruit bar for dinner, which was usually right around the time of his match. Mixing good fats with protein and a little burst of natural sugar always gave Kevin what he needed to excel.

Kevin believed in drinking water with his lunch and always during — and especially after — training. He also supported his nutrition regimen with key supplements, including a daily multivitamin and Juice Plus (a natural fruit and vegetable based supplement). He took Vitamin C to build his immune system and B12 for energy, helping him reach "utopia," his natural performance high.

On the day of competition, Kevin would fast, consuming only honey for energy, until he completed all divisions for the day. He would spend his time before and between events meditating and greeting others who would always be given a firm handshake and a bright, heartfelt smile. These physical, mental, emotional and spiritual disciplines done over a lifetime of competition allowed Kevin to compete for more than 40 years without any significant injury.

Tribute by Damon Gilbert

Where do I begin? It's hard to put into words what Kevin Thompson means to sport Karate. In my humble opinion Kevin is a true icon. He is our Willie Mayes, Bill Russell, Michael Jordan, or Joe Montana. Has there ever been another competitor who was a true triple threat in the men's division? I'm talking about forms, weapons, and fighting. Not just winning first place, but actually winning overall Grand Championships, many times over. The amount of focus, commitment, and endurance that Kevin has displayed over the decades is second to none. He may be the only person walking God's green earth that can say he won every major sport karate competition in forms, fighting, and weapons. On top of all that, Kevin has also been a member of sport karate's most prestigious teams (Budweiser, Team Paul Mitchell, etc.).

Kevin is the kind of competitor who made younger competitors like me look at him and wish to have even half the success that he earned.

I remember watching Kevin fight in 1994 at the Compete Classic in Los Angeles, California. He was fighting on Team Paul Mitchell. The energy and excitement that he displayed before the fight was something that I had never seen before. Kevin was pacing back and forth waiting for the referee to start the fight. Standing across the ring from Kevin was one of the iconic Brady twins from the Metro All Stars. As soon as the referee bowed in the fighters, Brady came off the line pumping kicks. Kevin stayed stationary, and when Brady got close, Kevin threw one of the most perfectly timed spinning back kicks I had ever seen. Next thing you know, Mr. Brady was on the ground.

The Paul Mitchell versus Metro All-Stars battles in the early '90s were truly legendary. And Kevin Thompson was right there in the middle of all of them. No one wore Paul Mitchell black and white like Kevin Thompson!

I always dreamed of having ankle-breaking angles like Kevin. Kevin's use of angles and making an opponent miss was second to none! I also loved Kevin's boxing skills. He was one of the first fighters who I saw bob and weave when he was mixing it up in the corner with much larger opponents. Kevin was the kind of fighter who actually hit his opponents. I have seen Kevin drop several fighters with his awesome basics. He has to be regarded as one of the most feared fighters of all time: power, speed, timing, and relentless will to win set him apart from many other fighters for four decades.

I am the biggest Kevin Thompson fan!!!! I love the way Kevin does his intro to the officials before performing his kata. I love that signature Kevin Thompson Kia! I even loved when Kevin wore the Jason from **Friday the 13th** *mask. I loved seeing Kevin perform his kata to Michael Jackson's "Bad." I loved* *being able to witness first-hand Kevin defeating multiple fighters half his age at the 2008 U.S. Open. Kevin went undefeated and shared the overall title with his teammate, Alex Lane. He has to be the oldest fighter to ever win that prestigious grand championship title.*

Kevin Thompson is the best teammate that I ever went into battle alongside.

I must admit that when I first joined Team Paul Mitchell I was nervous about being on the same team as a living legend. I assumed that Kevin would be distant and not have time to deal with a snot-nosed kid like me. But he was just the opposite. Kevin welcomed me onto the team with open arms, a big hug, and a hard smack on the butt. He took me under his wing. He was the best roommate a guy could ever have. I was blessed with an opportunity to observe the other side of this great martial artist. I also saw that he was a loving father and husband, a man of faith and religious values. And that he was a man of great integrity.

Kevin was the ultimate team captain, one that led by example. He was always behind me when I was fighting. He knew just how to motivate me and make me believe in myself. Kevin would simply look at me and say, "Let's go, D!" and smack me on the butt. Once he hit me, a surge of energy took over my body. All of the butterflies went away. How could I lack confidence when I had one of the greatest minds ever in sport karate coaching and leading me? Those times were priceless.

I guess some things don't change. It's 2014 and I still find myself wanting to be like Kevin Thompson. The strength, willpower and determination that Kevin displayed in light of recent setbacks are what I admire about him most.

My love, admiration, and respect only grows for Kevin as each day passes. I can never put into words how grateful I am that Don Rodrigues put me on the same team as the great Kevin Thompson.

Damon Gilbert, member and coach of Team Paul Mitchell Karate

13. THE BEGINNING OF THE END
OF COMPETITION

After playing a tennis match in the summer of 2008, Kevin's left leg gave him trouble, but he thought it was a hamstring injury and competed through the pain until the end of the karate season.

After the Diamond Nationals in Minneapolis, his doctor ordered an MRI, which showed a meniscus tear. Kevin allowed it time to heal by resting from Thanksgiving through the New Year. He watched holiday football games on the couch with his leg raised up on pillows.

To take the pressure off, Kevin switched his weapon from Kama to Sword and Bo. This enabled him to perform at the highest level without going into more strenuous deep stances, jump kicks and explosive movements that were required by his other forms. He continued competing and winning in this way despite his leg being wrapped for extra support — and even though he was aware of a lack of push off from his left leg.

Kevin also experienced problems blitzing forward and cutting angles. The explosiveness and angular movement that was his trademark was missing. It became especially apparent at the US Capital Classics in a match against Curt Pernell, when Kevin's mind told him what to do but his legs didn't respond.

"That's when I knew my rehab didn't go well," Kevin said.

What he didn't know yet was that his muscles had entered a slow, irreversible decline. The final tournament of the year in 2009, as it was every year, was the Diamond Nationals. Kevin won his division and then bowed out to his teammate — that was me — Chris Rappold.

As was the routine for all his years of competition, between the beginning of October through Thanksgiving, Kevin backed off his weekly routine and allowed his body time to rest and rejuvenate. The sport karate season was a long and arduous one, with top national and international competitions from January through the first week in October. The beginning of the next year's routine would always take root the Sunday after every Thanksgiving. Kevin attempted to develop a new routine in November 2009 and noticed himself shaking on the treadmill. He thought it odd but didn't give it much attention. Then it was stretching, push-ups, and sit-ups. Again Kevin felt his legs shaking. Ever determined to will his way out of something, he focused his mind, deepened his stances and was intent on sticking a deep stance. He gathered himself, let out a loud yell and tried to stick his stance really hard and for the first time completely lost his balance, his left leg trembling. The workout ended prematurely and he went upstairs to tell his wife Shena what happened.

It was the beginning of an awareness that something more than a strained hamstring or a torn meniscus was at play.

"I will get through this and get back to what I was doing," Kevin thought.

This began a two-year parade of doctors and neurologists, each trying to understand and get a handle on what was happening in Kevin's body.

Realizing he couldn't compete and represent himself and his team with the standard he demanded of himself, Kevin called Team Paul Mitchell Coach Don Rodrigues and announced that he would, after 40 years of steady competition, retire from the sport to which he had devoted his life. And Kevin, always the man of honor and respect, thought it most appropriate to announce his retirement at his coach's tournament — The Ocean State Grand Nationals.

14 T.E.A.M.

Never forget where you come from and who was there to support you along the way. First we were competitors then T.E.A.M.mates (Together Each Achieves More).

•••

To Kevin, "Team" was such a powerful word. Any two people coming together for a unified purpose was a team. He saw the power of team in everything. He marveled at the miracle of a procession of ants working all day in the hot sun, one line of them going one way, the other line going the other way, until their mutual goal was accomplished.

"We have no lack of example," Kevin said. "Everything that has been created has been created by a team — two or more."

Take a simple water bottle: Kevin would recognize in it that someone took the water from the ground, someone else transported it, still another person made the plastic bottle it went in, other people designed the look and advertised the brand, and still others were in charge of selling it.

"Team is about building a family. It's about fighting for someone else's pride and honor," he said. And he knew the team was bigger than just him. Kevin spoke of the sacredness of a team and gave reverence to the concept of team as most people speak and feel about their own flesh and blood.

As his Budweiser, Atlantic and Transworld Oil teams each came to an end and was replaced, the who's who of martial arts superstars stayed together, and, for an era in the 1980s, were untouchable. In the early '90s, Kevin found himself for the first time in years without a team. A number of squads pursued him, but Kevin knew and believed in the power of TEAM and took his time choosing which one to join.

He consulted with Chuck Merriman, his former coach on the Atlantic and Transworld Oil teams. Merriman said, "Kevin you are a man of character, go with Donnie (Don Rodrigues)." Kevin agreed with that recommendation. He could relate to Coach Rodrigues' humble beginnings. He knew from their conversations that Coach Rodrigues was loyal to the lessons his father had taught him as a boy and he knew that underneath the rough exterior was a man of intellect and knowledge, one that understood his own life and art. Kevin admired his work ethic and his commitment to providing for his family.

The decision was made... Team Paul Mitchell it was.

Kevin's belief in team came from the traditions he learned in his family, being raised in a traditional art and being a devout Muslim. As a player on the team, "You do as you are told, not as you want," he said. He recognized the power of sacrifice for the greater good of the team and if you choose to be on a team, your goal becomes the fulfillment of the team mission, through your character and performance. It wasn't enough to be number one in the standings; Kevin wanted each and every one of his teammates to be undefeated.

"You respect the rank of Black Belt or any belt for that matter," Kevin said. "You live within an environment where you request, you don't expect. In a workout, if you want to get a drink of water, you ask permission or wait for the break; you don't just walk off the floor. You never curse, because that becomes a reflection of who you are on the inside. When a higher rank enters a conversation, you give way to allow them into the conversation; you humble yourself and take a second position."

•••

With his own children, Kevin taught that when they came home from school — or if they were going out with friends — to first take the time to see mom and dad. Give a direct "Hello" and express your respect and reverence and think about the reason you are here. Similar to the way a person bows in martial arts, it should always be done in a way as to pause and think about to whom you are bowing. So often in a world of texting and being constantly on the go, it is easy to forget the importance taking a moment. Kevin told his children these things not out of ego but rather to foster an example.

"Your mom and I deserve and have earned the time to ask you questions and check in with you," he said.

Kevin believed in leading by example. He asked his children, "How can I tell the dog to stop barking if I haven't trained him?" — meaning it was up to him as a leader to set an example and create and train the expectation he wanted followed.

As a person who competed for four decades, he always carried himself outside the ring with humility. If you didn't know who he was, you would have assumed he was great when you looked at his physique and the confident mannerisms he embodied.

"The way you stand, greet someone, walk and talk should exhibit excellence at all times," Kevin said.

Having won more tournaments than anyone in the history of sport karate was not a reason for acting the part; he believed anyone who acted like that was only fooling themselves and being misled by a falsehood.

"Tournament is only a competition," he said. "Your mark and mindset should be towards making an example of excellence to all onlookers."

This example was extended to the way Team Paul Mitchell made decisions about player selection. Kevin remembered looking at one of the great fighters of the decade. In doing research into the person's background, he found something that raised questions about the person's character. Though the person was a top competitor, his character piece was flawed. "This team is not built on just skill," Kevin believed. "First and foremost, your character must be intact."

Kevin also brought an attitude of giving and sharing to make the team better. He had no tolerance for people who showed up to an event without proper training and preparation or who were just there to collect a paycheck.

"How do you build a team around jokers who don't show up or are here because John Paul Mitchell paid their way?" he asked.

Team, Kevin taught, had the potential of creating 1+1=3 power.

In the late 1980s, while on the Transworld Oil Karate Team, Kevin found himself in head-to-head competition in the traditional division against Gabe Renyaga from Team Paul Mitchell. Though they were close in performance, he felt the power of the team working against him. While Kevin performed, his teammates were back in the room still asleep. When Renyaga started, Kevin noticed a sea of black and white Team Paul Mitchell uniformed players around the ring cheering him on.

When Renyaga finished, Renyaga's Team Paul Mitchell mates around the ring erupted. In evenly matched competition, the positive influence of team members or spectators attempts to move the score in the minds of the judges from a 99.8 to a 99.9. The difference between first and second place can be literally one-hundredth of a point.

After that experience, Kevin used his influence to change the culture on the team to be present at all team members' rings whenever possible... no more sleeping in.

•••

At a tournament there are two parts of the participant's experience: competing in the events and back at the hotel with teammates. Over time, wins, losses, disappointments, defeats and setbacks are shared equally. There is much laughter and occasional tears. Team talk back in the hotel rooms and in training sessions allowed Kevin to be more strategic, more creative, more giving and mindful of all. It helped him see other people's viewpoints in the inevitable back and forth of opinions and perceptions of a day's events. Teammates shared insights and together they broke down fighters against whom they would compete. Because of his humility, he recognized that no matter how different an opinion was from his own, it was valid in its own right and provided good food for thought.

One of Kevin's teammates was Tony Young, who was among the best super lightweight fighters of all time.

Kevin and Tony both had children in the same year, making their bond and commonalities even deeper. They went back to their rooms earlier than most and stayed up for hours talking about family and the importance of winning "Diaper Money" the next day to take home. Together they feasted on tuna, bread and juice that they brought from home to save money instead of dining out.

Kevin never forgot that having a professional sponsor was rare in the sport of karate. John Paul Dejoria, founder of The Paul Mitchell System, made a long-term commitment to the team and its players that was a greatly appreciated gift. As a result, Kevin was focused on giving back to his sport and instilling through example and occasional lecture with the command of a preacher, the importance of following the principles of honor, commitment and integrity, the ingredients upon which Team Paul Mitchell was founded. He enjoyed being part of making a statement at the start of each event as people and other teams walked in one at a time to be part of a unified wave of black and white all entering together.

It was the notion of paying tribute to the commitment of John Paul Dejoria, his company, its coaching staff and players that motivated Kevin.

"You should willingly give with the generosity of your heart all the love, support and care you can to your team," Kevin said.

He connected to that notion and was proud to be a part of it.

As he looked at the word "Karate," Kevin's interpretation of the word broke it down into two parts: "Kara," to empty yourself fully and to give of one's heart and mind — and "Te," the hand to do the work and put something back into the heart and mind.

While others were focused on winning trophies, Kevin focused on using his labor to empty himself fully and make the people around him better.

Tribute by Caitlin Dechelle

You have achieved so much in your competition years. You are such an idol and role model to everyone on the team, as well as other competitors on the circuit. You have set such a high standard for everyone to follow and I applaud you for that. Your spirit will always be in each one of us.

Caitlin Dechelle, member of Team Paul Mitchell Karate, actor

15. ALS IS A GIFT

To most of us, it is hard to wrap our heads around ALS being a gift. It was certainly difficult for Kevin Thompson.

What exactly *is* ALS? I borrowed the following explanation from the ALS Association's website[1]:

> **Amyotrophic lateral sclerosis (ALS) is a progressive neurodegenerative disease that affects nerve cells in the brain and the spinal cord. Motor neurons reach from the brain to the spinal cord and from the spinal cord to the muscles throughout the body. The progressive degeneration of the motor neurons in ALS eventually leads to their death. When the motor neurons die, the ability of the brain to initiate and control muscle movement is lost. With voluntary muscle action progressively affected, patients in the later stages of the disease may become totally paralyzed.**

Most people know of ALS through its other name: Lou Gehrig's Disease, so named for the legendary New York Yankees baseball player who was struck down in his prime by it.

The ALS Association reports that Gehrig was hardly the last athlete or celebrity struck by ALS; other victims include Hall of Fame pitcher Jim "Catfish" Hunter, Senator Jacob Javits, actors Michael Zaslow and David Niven, creator of Sesame Street Jon Stone, television producer Scott Brazil, boxing champion Ezzard Charles, NBA Hall of Fame basketball player George Yardley, pro football player Glenn Montgomery, golfer Jeff Julian, golf caddie Bruce Edwards, British soccer player Jimmy Johnstone, musician Lead Belly (Huddie

---

[1] http://www.alsa.org/about-als/

Ledbetter), photographer Eddie Adams, entertainer Dennis Day, jazz musician Charles Mingus, composer Dimitri Shostakovich, former vice president of the United States Henry A. Wallace and U.S. Army General Maxwell Taylor.

The chances of someone contracting ALS are 1-in-500,000. Presently, the disease does not have a cure. One's lifestyle takes a dramatic shift from independence to requiring the support of loved ones for simple day-to-day activities. It has opened up a new world to Kevin; an emerging one of love and respect from a generation that he influenced and impacted over his 52 years as an example of excellence.

Kevin could have been taken from us in a car accident, plane crash (considering his extensive travel for so many decades), suffered a heart attack or some other tragedy to end his life. His joy of living and being with his family, friends, work colleagues and team could have ended abruptly without a good-bye or properly expressed appreciation. Instead, Kevin enjoys the rare sight of his impact on people from his lifetime of dedication and example setting.

When talk among the doctors started around the subject of ALS, quite frankly, Kevin spiraled into depression. The reality was too big and he didn't know how to express it to people. Always the warrior, he withdrew and — while seeking answers — sought to tap into the unfamiliar humility of admitting a weakness, something that for a person who devoted his entire life to the perfection of his physical body was foreign territory. He went into a period of complete withdrawal from the outside world. He needed to come to terms with it prior to sharing this unfortunate development with the public.

Fortunately for all the people who loved and cared about Kevin, his mind, his heart and his selflessness for others won out as he came to terms with the importance of letting others share this journey with him.

Kevin started the process by reaching out to those closest to him.

Call by call, he came to terms with admitting to others what at first was hard to admit to himself; something he wasn't able to control or fix had brought his physical body, the once perfect weapon, into a state of decline. And while the physical burden was his to bear, the mental, emotional and physical connection of 52 years of relationships started a life of its own and rays of sun started to shine through.

With the same determination of pounding his training gravel, Kevin believes with every fiber of his being about the importance of still laughing with the kids and enjoying the love and companionship with his wife, though date nights now are more confined to dinner and super-slow dancing on the back porch. He embraces the advice of the legendary North Carolina State University basketball coach Jim "Jimmy V" Valvano, who reminded us each and every day to think, laugh, and be emotional.

Students, coworkers, martial arts promoters, competitors, team members, former team members, and rival competitors from all over the country have poured their hearts out to the humble warrior who gave them so much, individually and collectively.

The high school where Kevin Thompson was an assistant principal initiated an annual scholarship in his name. Former students created events in Kevin's honor to demonstrate their love and respect for his influence upon them. Martial artists came together in tribute to Kevin and to raise funds for his treatment. The attention befit a person who devoted his life to excellence, but who probably wasn't aware of the impact he created.

Even if you don't know Kevin, you could always tell the kind of person he is by viewing all the people that have come out to support him and give him the respect due for a lifetime of inspiration. To some, he is the living, breathing, bigger-than-life inspiration that Bruce Lee was for a previous generation.

Kevin's historic achievement of being a top forms, fighting and weapon competitor for four decades stands as a record that has no equal and in all likelihood will never be broken.

He amassed this through time-honored, hard physical and mental discipline accrued over a lifetime. He did it with the ferocity in the ring of a caged, hungry tiger and with the humility of a servant leader outside the ring.

Ever the warrior, Kevin continues to do battle each day with ALS. He uses his celebrity to shine a light on the disease by taking his message to the halls of the U.S. Congress, where he spoke on behalf of the ALS Foundation for Life (www.ALSFoundation.org) to ask for more research money to find a cure. He was also an honoree at Yankee Stadium in July 2014 to commemorate the 75th anniversary of Lou Gehrig's famous farewell speech, in which the man dubbed "The Iron Horse" said,

"Today, I consider myself the luckiest man on the face of the earth." As Kevin continues his own battle with ALS, we hope that in his heart, he feels the same.

To know Kevin Thompson is to come face to face with the possibilities and potential that is the best in all of us.

And in Kevin's own words, "Everything you are giving in tribute for me for has happened because all of you were there with me allowing it to happen, so I say... Thank you."

Tribute by Matt Emig

While in the hospital for 10 days, feeling very down, in a lot of pain and depressed, it was hard to pick myself up. On the day that I was finally going home, I was a little excited but my spirits still were not good. As I checked my phone messages, I found one from Kevin Thompson. Listening to his voicemail put a huge smile on my face. Kevin's encouragement meant more to me than he will ever know. His words gave me hope and happiness that I hadn't felt since before being hospitalized.

I never told anyone this but during the next three weeks I listened to Kevin's voicemail a dozen times. Each and every time he put a smile on my face, got me pumped up and ready to face the challenges ahead.

Matt Emig, member of Team Paul Mitchell Karate, actor

Tribute by Joe Corley

When Kevin Thompson's name comes up in any conversation, I picture his big, room-warming smile, followed by a pain in my right hand from his handshake. I immediately think of the power that came through his hand in that simple greeting.

My mind then goes to his focused fierceness in forms, manipulating weapons, and in manhandling the thousands of hapless opponents he faced in the ring.

In my book, he was a living example of how martial arts warriors are supposed to be. Straight forward, dangerous, yet humble. He also brought a huge dose of persistence.

I think often of "Little K.A." when we were in Madison Square Garden 30 years ago, and I flash to the 18-29s, the 30-39s and the executives — K.T. is champion in all of those visions.

I always admired him, from close and afar. He deserved the best because that's what he always gave us.

Joe Corley is the CEO of PKA Warriors and founder of "Battle of Atlanta"

Tribute by Abdul Mutakabbir

This is a letter that ALLAH INSPIRED me to write to our brother I share with you!

My beloved brother, I think of you often and hear your warrior cry as you are doing kata and kumite in my mind. I stop and say to myself, "That's the yell of my beloved brother, "Little KA," Kevin Thompson, the 8th Wonder of the World, one of the greatest martial artists produced by the East Coast, whose journey continues to inspire the young and old.

As one warrior to another, I pray for you that ALLAH makes it expedient in your recovery. Man does not have all the answers in life's mystification. Only ALLAH can make all things new, including you!

So keep your faith, discipline, and patience and watch ALLAH do his work on you.

Who knows, maybe He will use you as the cure for the disease, you ARE known as the 8th Wonder!

Forever, I walk by your side.

Your beloved brother in faith, Abdul Mutakabbir

16. FINAL THOUGHTS

Sport martial artist Billy Beason was consistently the most challenging foe that Kevin Thompson ever faced. I thought his perspective on Kevin's career and life sums up his story best.

Here's what Billy had to say in tribute to Kevin:

I was just a 14-year-old Brown Belt when I saw the magazine article about this kid, Kevin Thompson. With him living in New Jersey, just a stone's throw away from the Bronx, New York, it made me nervous, since I had recently started competing in karate tournaments. It was only a matter of time before we would come face to face. So, when I first met Kevin Thompson, there was no pleasant introduction – I was about 13 and so was he. It went more like this:

"*Hmmm...* So that's him."

That was it... nothing else. I just saw him and watched him as if he were prey.

He was smaller than I had imagined. After all, I was expecting someone larger than life. You see, at the ripe old age of 14, Kevin Thompson was a seasoned veteran and already labeled "The Eighth Wonder of the World" by the legendary Aaron Banks, in recognition of his amazing abilities as a youngster.

Kevin walked in with his entourage, all gi'd up, white gi, colorful school emblems all over the gi, hands menacingly wrapped and taped. But what I most remember about him was this silly little headband he wore. Scary bunch of dudes these K.A. dudes were, I thought. I'm sure he didn't notice me at all.

We didn't fight the first few times we saw each other. I don't really recall the details. However, at some point, I must have gotten his attention, because I remember that he and his boys approached me and surrounded me in the locker room at a tournament. Kevin came into the inner circle of this group where I was, looked me up and down and said, "Hmmph!" He was indicating I was nothing, then they walked away. Those K.A. boys loved to intimidate people!

I don't remember being intimidated, or being afraid... I don't even remember if I told anyone about the incident at the time. I just knew now, from my standpoint, it was on!

We finally met in competition for the first time in 1975 at a tournament on Staten Island, New York. It was the nighttime finals; the top three Super Juniors that night were Kevin Thompson, a.k.a., Little K.A., Robert Wright, a.k.a., Mr. Graceful, and me, Billy Beason.

I had to make a statement at that moment and I did. I wanted to knock that silly headband off his head, and I did. Further details of the fight are, of course, blurry and not important. After all, it was 38 years ago. What is important, however, is that once that fire was lit, it would change our lives for decades to come.

Had Kevin beaten me that night and the next tournament and the next, so on and so forth, we wouldn't really have a story here. I would have been just another kid in the division. But I did win that first encounter. You see, Little K.A. didn't lose – to anyone! This wasn't supposed to happen... especially from me, this new kid on the tournament scene.

However, what we had now was a rivalry, which was fuel for our personal training practices as well... When I would train, I had Kevin Thompson in mind. When my arm got weary from bag work, when my kicks got sloppy in practice, when I fought my dojo brothers, I yelled out in my mind "*K.A.! BAMMM!*" with each blow to the bag or with each opponent I faced. I practiced with increasing power, form and intensity, because I knew if I could get past Kevin Thompson, the rest would come easy. I trained harder – just to beat *him.*

I didn't realize until years later that Kevin was on the opposite side of the Hudson River with the same mental attitude...we've since talked about that kind of training, and were amazingly intrigued that we drove each other in that way!

It was during these formative years that we pushed each other to a higher level.

Over the years, from 1975 to 1992, we fought between 35 and 40 times and the record is unclear as to who won more times. Actually there is no record; open karate tournaments never kept such records, so it can never be verified. I used to say that I won more. Kevin would answer by telling me, "Yeah, you did... in your dreams!"

What was important was how we grew from young men and rivals to grown men and friends. And not just friends or acquaintances, but good and dear friends — the kind of friend who even if you haven't seen for years, when you do see each other after all that passage of time, it seems like it's only been a week. The kind of friend with who time doesn't erase affection. The kind of friend that was always ready when called upon.

Kevin and I bonded in a way that neither of us understood. In spite of the rivalry, in spite of the dojo affiliations, in spite of the opposing teams we were on, in spite of those biased supporters who only saw the surface relationship, we went outside of that part of our lives and learned about each other as people.

A level of respect and mutual admiration developed and has stood the passage of time and we have had some effect on each other's lives.

Kevin went on to be a great, great, great champion, indisputably one of the best to ever enter the open tournament circuit. He is a fantastic husband to his wife, Shena, and great father to his son, Kevin Jr., and his daughter, Kashea. He is a great teacher in his dojo as well as a respected educator in his secular career, and just a generally all-around great guy, positive to everyone, one that makes you feel important even if he doesn't actually know your name.

What more can I say? All of his endeavors indicate that he has mastered life, and indeed should be known as a grandmaster because of all aspects of life, not only his martial arts, but because of his humanity.

When Kevin told me that he might be seriously ill, I had a visceral reaction, that feeling you get when something happens to a close family member and, months later, when it was confirmed, I was deeply saddened and angry at the diagnosis.

How could a champion like Kevin, a man so physically fit, so conscious of his physical nature, a man who never engaged in any bad habits, be afflicted so?

Respecting my dear friend's confidentiality, I kept silent until I heard that the information had been publicly revealed, yet I still refrained from discussing details of my friend's business.

Sonny Williams, Aziz Abdul and I put into action a campaign to raise funds to help this great warrior any way we could.

However, the more important need that I recognize is that I must support my "rival" in any way that I can, by text, calls or pictures, thoughts or prayer. And I recognized the need for others to do the same. Let Kevin know how important he is to us as a person, let him know how proud we are of him that he represented the New Jersey/New York area well for so many decades on the open tournament circuit.

Who would have thought that two teenagers, with great abilities for their age, two young men who once smashed fists into each other, two grown men who would do their very best to be victorious over the other, would one day call each other "brother"?

The one regret that I have is that before my departure from the martial arts was that we had not done one thing — and that was to train together. Go into the dojo, close and lock the door and learn from each other. Kevin seems to thinks that he might have even been better — I couldn't imagine Kevin any better! I know that he would have made *me* better.

Just recently, someone asked me, "How can men who fight each other so hard hug each other after the match?"

I answered, "A champion recognizes another champion and knows what it took to get into that ring. They know what sacrifices were made, they know the physical pain that they went through, they know the hard work that was done. In one word, respect."

K.A. boy!
K.A. boy!
You look so sweet!
You know you can't be beat!

This was a rhyme chanted back in the day... by Kevin's dojo members.

When I think of Kevin, I always see that big cheesy smile and hear this song in my head.

K.A. boy! K.A. boy!
Rumble young man
Rumble!

75

17 PHOTO GALLERY

The photographs of Kevin Thompson on the pages that follow representing a sampling of the friends he has made, the classes and students he has taught, the teams on which he has competed, and the place that his sport martial arts journey has taken him.

Two sport karate legends Kevin Thompson and Billy Blanks. Billy later retired from sport competition and is most famous for being the creator of Tae Bo.

Taking time out for a photo with actor Leo Fung in California in 1982

Kevin devoted his life to martial arts and passing on its tradition of honor and integrity to the next generation. Here he is in 2008 awarding rank to a deserving youngster.

The Atlantic Karate Team in Russia circa 1987.

Team Paul Mitchell photograph with actor Chuck Norris (back row, fifth from left) at the Ocean State Grand Nationals in 1999. Kevin was an active competitor on team Paul Mitchell from 1993 till his retirement in 2009. Kevin Thompson or his initials KA or #KASTRONG signify the highest standard of excellence inside and outside the ring to our team members.

Instilling precision and high energy Kevin at his Dojo with his demo team in 2005.

In 1986, the greatest assembling of sport karate competitors under one banner… the Atlantic Karate team.

Pictured from left to right, fighting greats Anthony Price,
Richard Plowden, and Steve "Nasty" Anderson

Kevin training in the dojo with his then 7-year-old son Kevin Jr. (KJ)

Team Paul Mitchell Coach Don Rodrigues and Kevin
take time out to pose for a picture.

Kevin preparing his 4-year-old daughter KeShea for a demonstration

After-school promotion at East Orange Charter School, 2007

(L-R) Kevin's brother Earl, Kevin, and brother Milo in 1983 at the
Norwalk Y.M.C.A., celebrating Kevin being honored for his work
in the community.

W.A.K.O. USA Team in Italy in 1990 competing among 65 other
countries for top honors of being crowned World Champion

Fellow World Champions Kevin Thompson and New York Yankees
Team Captain Derek Jeter at the 75th anniversary celebration of Lou
Gehrig's legendary "I am the luckiest man" speech, 2014.

ABOUT THE AUTHOR
CHRISTOPHER M. RAPPOLD

Christopher Rappold holds a 6th Degree Black Belt in Karate and is a five-time World Champion who retired from competition in 2011 and now served as Executive Director for Team Paul Mitchell Karate.

A graduate of Bridgewater State College with a degree in Physical Education, he represented the United States of America as a top athlete in his sport many times over the years. In both 1995 and 1997, Rappold was awarded the prestigious "Martial Artist of the Year Award" and has been inducted into several Halls of Fame.

He was honored locally as "Business Person of the Year" by the Chamber of Commerce and recognized as a 50th Medallion Winner at Cardinal Spellman High School. In celebration of its 50-year anniversary, the school commemorated Rappold as being one of the "50 Most Influential People" to graduate Cardinal Spellman.

Rappold has studied the martial arts since 1982 and earned the title of Master Instructor in 1995. Being a student of the art, he has had the opportunity to study with some of the finest martial arts practitioners in the world. His intensive and continuous study brings his students and team members the best of what is available. As the Founder of Personal Best Karate, based in Norton, Massachusetts, Rappold took the attributes that made him a success in competition and integrated them with outstanding operational systems learned from the top 2% in the industry. This has allowed Personal Best Karate to enjoy a well respected national reputation.

As an active community leader, he continues to extend his positive influence not only in the schools, but also throughout the community. Rappold currently champions an anti-bully program, in 30 local schools. Additionally, he is the founder of Personal Best Charity. The major event for the charity, under the direction of Rappold, is its annual Thanksgiving Turkey Brigade. Begun in 1996, the effort provides full meals to over 3000 families each year. Rappold also created a program at

Personal Best to provide partial and full tuition scholarships to at risk children. Rappold's efforts on behalf of so many people have been recognized both locally as a "Friends of Children" award winner and most famously by his representation as an Olympic Torch Bearer.

He is professional speaker who shares his motivational outlook on life with audiences from all walks of life. Rappold is also an active writer and speaker in the martial arts industry.

To contact the author, please email him founder@personalbestkarate.com

19063039R00057

Made in the USA
Middletown, DE
02 April 2015